© Greg Martin

GEORGE PACKER

BETRAYED

GEORGE PACKER is a staff writer for *The New Yorker* and the author of five books, including *Blood of the Liberals* (FSG, 2000), winner of the 2001 Robert F. Kennedy Award, and, most recently, *The Assassins' Gate* (FSG, 2005), which was a *New York Times* Best Book of the Year. He is also the editor of the anthology *The Fight Is for Democracy* and was a 2001–2002 Guggenheim Fellow. His reporting has won four Overseas Press Club awards. He lives in Brooklyn. *Betrayed* is his first play.

ALSO BY GEORGE PACKER

NONFICTION

The Village of Waiting
Blood of the Liberals
The Assassins' Gate

FICTION

The Half Man
Central Square

AS EDITOR

The Fight Is for Democracy:
Winning the War of Ideas in America and the World

BETRAYED

BETRAYED

GEORGE PACKER

FABER AND FABER, INC.
An affiliate of FARRAR, STRAUS AND GIROUX / NEW YORK

FABER AND FABER, INC.
An affiliate of Farrar, Straus and Giroux
18 West 18th Street, New York 10011

Library of Congress Cataloging-in-Publication Data
Packer, George, 1960–
    Betrayed / George Packer.— 1st ed.
      p.   cm.
    ISBN-13: 978-0-86547-991-3 (pbk. : alk. paper)
    ISBN-10: 0-86547-991-7 (pbk. : alk. paper)
    1. Translators—Iraq—Drama.   2. Iraq War, 2003—Drama.
  3. Americans—Iraq—Drama.   I. Title.

PS3566.A317B48 2008
812'.54—dc22

                                                    2007047949

Designed by Gretchen Achilles

www.fsgbooks.com

1   3   5   7   9   10   8   6   4   2

For the Iraqis who gave me their words—Ameer, Ayad, Ban,
Ehab, Firas, Hossam, Intisar, Laith, Mwaffaq, Omer, Tona,
and Yaghdan—and for Kirk Johnson

INTRODUCTION

In January 2007 I went to Iraq for the sixth time since the beginning of the war. My idea was to write an article for *The New Yorker* about Iraqis who had worked with the Americans in their country—that tiny minority of mostly young men and women who had embraced the American project in Iraq so enthusiastically that they were willing to risk their lives for it. By then they were not easy to meet: one of them, from southern Iraq, would talk to me only in Kurdistan, a plane ride away; two others insisted on taking a room in the bleak, nearly empty Palestine Hotel in central Baghdad for our conversations; some would meet only in the Green Zone, and others refused to go there; some could speak only by telephone because there simply was no safe way to be together. Others had scattered outside Iraq for safety, and I had to track them down in far-flung cities: Amman, Damascus, even Malmö, Sweden. I spoke with thirty or forty of these Iraqis, having long since learned that, when they are not too intimidated by dictators or insurgents, Iraqis are wonderful talkers. Over the course of these interviews a single overwhelming story emerged.

They were all leading precarious, furtive lives, using assumed names, limiting their contacts to a handful of trusted people, creating elaborate lies about their history and employment, afraid every time the phone rang or someone knocked on the door. Every one of them had good reason to believe that he or she could be killed at any time: it would just take one mistake—being seen by the wrong person at the Green Zone gate, uttering a few words of English in public, an embassy badge discovered at a police checkpoint—for the end to come. In the world's most violent country, they had no protectors. Every armed Iraqi faction, including the United States–supported government, saw them as traitors. Their American employers in general regarded their welfare as a bureaucratic nuisance. To survive, they had either to live entirely on American turf in Iraq, to establish double lives and move about as easy targets, or to leave the country. Normal existence in their homeland was impossible, and it would remain impossible for years—maybe for the rest of their lives. These Iraqis were as hunted and helpless as European Jews in the early 1940s. Conversations with them, which—once we could find a reasonably secure place to talk—lasted hours or even days, made my eyes burn with shame.

It wasn't just the dangerous circumstances of their lives that riveted me. In the stories they told one saw the larger course of the war, and in every individual version it was a trajectory from suffering to hope—the kind of dazzling, outsize hope that comes when, as several Iraqis put it, your world is a prison and someone suddenly opens the door—through a slow, reluctant, increasingly brutal process of disillusionment to a sense of abandonment and betrayal. For me, this was the essential experience of the Iraq war, and nowhere was it more vivid than in these lives, these stories. They had the most to gain from the overthrow of Saddam Hussein—they were young and modern enough to benefit from joining the wider world—and they lost the most when they became pariahs and outcasts in their own society. They had pinned their hopes, irrationally it turned out, on the Americans, until those Americans proved to be not just incompetent occupiers but also unreliable allies and indifferent friends. But the tone of the stories was never simply bitter, as one might have expected; it was closer to the lingering surprise and hurt of a jilted lover. These Iraqis still spoke fondly of Americans and America. Every Iraqi knew an American who had tried, within the bureaucratic limits of the civilian and military structures in Iraq, to help someone in danger. The help was almost never enough: the American eventually left and the connection became tenuous, with no institutional means to oblige the U.S. government to honor its commitment to its best friends in Iraq, while the Iraqi continued to dodge death every day.

I wrote the article, which was published under the title "Betrayed" in the March 26, 2007, issue of *The New Yorker*. Usually that's the end of the story, but not in this case. The words that had filled my recorder continued to haunt me. They had the inadvertent bluntness and accidental poetry of a second language, and the intensity of life caught in a reflective pause during an extreme time. They spoke of great hope and equally great disappointment, and they tapped directly into feelings that the war evoked in me, as in many other Americans who became involved—guilt and anger, but deeper than these, a terrible sense of loss. They expressed what had always interested me most about the war: how the Americans and Iraqis saw one another, what kind of relationship was possible in such violent circumstances, the ability or inability of individuals to transcend their "official" roles and maintain a human pulse. In my experience this relationship defied the propaganda of all sides—it was neither that of liberator and liberated nor that of oppressor and oppressed. There was far too much mutual need and mutual suspicion, expectation and ignorance, simple affection and simple hatred, desperation and pain, to conform to the slogans and certainties of the war's far-off judges.

In the spring of 2007 a young director wrote to me to suggest that "Betrayed," with its handful of characters and inherent drama, might be the basis for a play. Soon afterward, I met the staff of Culture Project, a theater company in lower Manhattan that takes on topical new work, and when I ran the idea by them they were encouraging. The thought of writing a play was deeply appealing: it would offer the chance to return to an early passion. When I was around twelve, my burning ambition was to become a Shakespearean actor, and I wrote a letter to my hero, Laurence Olivier, asking for advice. He wrote back, essentially, "Don't," which was how things turned out. What I loved about theater was the experience of collaboration, with months of preparation leading up to spontaneous, unpredictable life onstage. Journalism, however much it means immersion in the world, isn't terribly less lonely in the writing than fiction. But with drama, the point at which other kinds of writing end is just when things start to get interesting. And rather than having to speak indirectly through a journalist, the Iraqis would get to speak for themselves (though the journalist wouldn't entirely disappear).

I sketched out the structure of a plot, basing it on a couple of incidents described in the magazine article, while allowing myself wide latitude to invent. The story needed to be intimate—a tale told by two men in a hotel room—and yet encompass the arc of the whole war. The characters—three leading Iraqi roles and one American—became, almost naturally, composites of people I'd interviewed. As for the dialogue, it all but wrote itself. I had the best possible source of spoken words—my interviews—and knew them well enough that, while writing, I could open the relevant transcript and quickly find the right line or passage for a particular scene. At least half the dialogue comes from life; it would have been foolish to try to improve on how the Iraqis spoke and what they said. When the script was finished in midsummer, Culture Project agreed to produce *Betrayed* at its theater in Soho in January 2008.

The titles of recent New York and London productions suggest that audiences are hungry for drama drawn from the news of our turbulent age. The intensity of feeling about current events apparently demands something more personal and cathartic than a television clip; a part of the public wants its news with the immediacy and vitality of dramatic art. Unfortunately, a lot of topical theater is short on art and long on indignation, as if standards of drama can be waived when a play comes wrapped in political good intentions. What an audience then feels is likely to be a letdown: the soothing ratification of its convictions rather than the disturbance of new ideas and emotions. I have strong views about the fate of America's Iraqi allies, who remain nearly as abandoned and endangered as when I first went to find them, and I wouldn't have taken the time to write a play about them if their plight didn't anger me. But what begins in partisanship can't end there, or the result will be bad writing and bad politics. By giving my characters living words, with their sudden exposure of the speaker's soul, I hoped to avoid the tendency toward flatness and cliché that is the occupational hazard of writing about contemporary issues. I wanted to do justice to the texture of life among Iraqi interpreters in wartime Baghdad in a way that can't be conveyed in a news article or even a feature story. I wanted the characters to surprise American audiences, not by being exotic but by being, in their specificity, familiar. For all these reasons, *Betrayed* owes more to the people named on its dedication page than simply the author's gratitude.

BETRAYED

PRODUCTION HISTORY

Betrayed had its world premiere at Culture Project at 55 Mercer Street in New York City on February 4, 2008. Founder and Artistic Director of Culture Project: Allan Buchman. Director: Pippin Parker. General Manager: David Friedman. Producer: Julianne Hoffenberg. Set and Lighting Designer: Garin Marschall. Sound Designer: Eric Shim. Production Manager: Garin Marschall. Stage Manager: Leanne L. Long.

ADNAN *Waleed F. Zuaiter*

LAITH *Sevan Greene*

CURSING MAN *Ramsey Faragallah*

SOLDIER *Jeremy Beck*

WOMAN *Aadya Bedi*

OLD MAN *Ramsey Faragallah*

DISHDASHA MAN *Ramsey Faragallah*

PRESCOTT *Michael Doyle*

RSO *Jeremy Beck*

INTISAR *Aadya Bedi*

EGGPLANT FACE *Ramsey Faragallah*

AMBASSADOR *Ramsey Faragallah*

N.B.: At the time this edition went to press, the roles of the First, Second, Third, and Fourth Correspondents had not yet been cast.

CHARACTERS

ADNAN *A young Sunni from western Baghdad*

LAITH *A young Kurdish Shia from Sadr City*

CURSING MAN

SOLDIER *An Army private from Indiana who stands duty at the Assassins' Gate*

WOMAN

OLD MAN

DISHDASHA MAN

PRESCOTT *A junior foreign service officer from Missouri, posted at the U.S. embassy in Baghdad*

RSO *The regional security officer, responsible for diplomatic security at the U.S. embassy in Baghdad*

INTISAR *A young woman from a secular Iraqi family*

EGGPLANT FACE

AMBASSADOR *The senior official at the U.S. embassy in Baghdad*

FIRST CORRESPONDENT

SECOND CORRESPONDENT

THIRD CORRESPONDENT

FOURTH CORRESPONDENT

SCENE ONE

A dark, spare hotel room in Baghdad, furnished in the soulless style of the Baathist era. The lights come up on two Iraqi men of about thirty sitting in chairs facing an unseen interviewer situated ostensibly among the audience. ADNAN *is soft-spoken, reflective, but quietly passionate;* LAITH *is more excitable and fidgety, with a hipper style. Next to* LAITH *is an old-fashioned Samsonite-type suitcase. On the table between them sits a small recorder with its LED light on.*

ADNAN So you made it. We were starting to worry. Did you have a problem with hotel security?

LAITH They didn't even search us. "Are you carrying any weapons? Okay, go." I could have a bomb under my shirt! This place is no longer safe like when the Americans had a tank in front of the hotel.

ADNAN But it's safer than any other place in Baghdad.

LAITH Because the foreigners are gone and it is not worth attacking.

ADNAN I wanted to offer you food, but the restaurant is closed. This is something really shameful for an Iraqi.

LAITH I think we're the only guests here. The manager

was so surprised to see us. At least there's hot water. I didn't take a hot shower for five weeks.

ADNAN Can you believe, my house is five kilometers away and it took me three days to get here? First there was fighting in Amiriya between the Americans and al Qaeda. They beheaded a teacher on my street. Then I got stuck at my sister's in Amel because the Mahdi Army was burning Sunni houses. My sister is married to a Shia man and he had to walk with me out to the road past the militia fighters to find a taxi. Without him they would have eaten me for breakfast. Do you know what is *alaasa*?

LAITH They are the informers who sit all day in the street and watch for people they consider the enemy. It means "the ones who chew."

ADNAN We have a new vocabulary.

LAITH (*Slightly embarrassed*) By the way, were you able to get the number? Ah, *shokran*, thank you so much. What is it? (*He dials the number on his cell phone.*)

ADNAN (*After a pause, touching the recorder*) Well . . . you said you wanted to hear the whole story, from the beginning of the war. That seems like such a long time ago.

LAITH (*Holding up his phone*) No network. Of course.

ADNAN Okay, since we have no food to offer, we will give you our story. You are free to ask us anything.

LAITH From the horse's mouth. (*He loves these American idioms.*)

ADNAN Only don't use my real name.

LAITH Or mine. Call me Laith.

ADNAN Why don't you give a more Shia name?

LAITH Why should I give a Shia name? Why talk about Sunni and Shia? You bring it up so much these days! I think you are becoming sectarian.

ADNAN He knows I'm not sectarian, or I would hand him over to al Qaeda because they control my street. But these days the first thing everyone wants to know is "Are you Sunni or Shia?" And if you give the wrong answer— (*He makes a slashing gesture across his throat.*)

LAITH You didn't give a name yet.

ADNAN Well, let's say Adnan.

LAITH Not very Sunni! His real name is the most totally Sunni name.

ADNAN This is my problem. I have to carry a fake ID for different parts of Baghdad.

LAITH Sometimes I feel like we're standing in line for a ticket, waiting to die.

Outside, the call to evening prayer begins. ADNAN *gets up and goes to look out the window, lights a cigarette, and smokes.* LAITH *is playing with his cell phone, nervously jiggling a leg. From time to time throughout the play he punches in the number again, with no luck.*

LAITH You know, when the Americans came to Baghdad this hotel wasn't empty and dark like now. Every Iraqi who wanted a job was here. Journalists were here, soldiers were here, everyone mixing freely. It's sad to remember, with all the hopes that we had, and all the dreams, after the invasion—

ADNAN I was totally against the word "invasion." Wherever I went I was defending the Americans and strongly saying America was here to make a change. But now I have my doubts.

LAITH Me the same.

ADNAN *smoking, beginning to remember.*

ADNAN During the war with Iran, I was listening to American songs, and I watched a lot of American movies on television. I loved the English language because I believed that to learn English opens horizons for you. In Saddam's time, everything was banned. So to put your hand on an English book, it tells you things you don't read in Arabic books, especially the Arabic books that managed to get to the market in Baghdad. But an English book, they didn't understand, they were ignorant people at that time, so an English book would pass. I read mostly philosophy and adventure books. To be totally frank with you, even some porn books. And this helped a lot to improve my English, because it's an interesting subject so you really make an effort to understand.

LAITH Everyone thought he was a little weird. Even his own family.

ADNAN One of the authors I read—Colin Wilson, a British existentialist—he wrote about the "non-belonger." So I always thought of myself as I don't belong to the society. It was a painful kind of existence. After university I couldn't get a government job, I was selling cigarettes, selling spare parts, selling books on Mutanabi Street. But there was always, always this sound in the back of my head: the time will come, the time will come, the change will come. My time will come. It is not my destiny to live and die in Iraq like this. And when 2003 came, I couldn't believe how right I was.

LAITH A week before the war, I saw Adnan in the barbershop. I was getting my haircut for the military. At that time I worked in a computer shop, and I was going to hide at home instead of going to fight. You know the string Iraqi barbers use to take off the small hairs of the beard? (*He demonstrates.*)

ADNAN I tied one string around his finger. (LAITH *shows his ring finger with the string.*) I told him, "You should remember me by this if I'm killed in the war."

LAITH But then it was over so fast. The Americans came and saved me. And at that time everyone was so happy.

ADNAN Imagine, overnight you can say anything you like about Saddam. The first day, on the ninth of April, that day I still remember it very clearly when I saw the first man who is in the middle of the street and cursing Saddam.

A CURSING MAN *steps into the light, ill dressed and poor looking, waving a photo of Saddam.*

CURSING MAN Saddam, you dog, you destroyed my life! You sent me to fight the Iranians and see what they did to me! (*He holds up his shirt to show a wound.*) For what? For you? Now I'm old, my life is finished. I spit on you, I step on your face! May the Americans catch you and cut you into a thousand pieces! May they destroy your sons and their sons forever! (*He puts the photo on the ground and stamps on it over and over until the light goes out.*)

ADNAN This is the new life that was revealing in front of us. At that time to see the Americans, whom we only saw in movies, in our streets (*the sound of Humvees roaring by and American voices,* "Salaam aleikum!" "*Get out of the way!*")—at that time you can speak freely about Saddam—at that time you discovered this hidden greed inside Iraqis when they started to loot their own country. (*Crowd noises, a mob scene*) Everything was shocking.

LAITH I saw Adnan and said, "Let's go to the Palestine Hotel. This is our chance!" To be frank with you, my reason was selfish. I was thinking of making a good salary and getting hired by an international technology company. But Adnan didn't want to go with me.

ADNAN This is my nature. I like to study a situation before I jump. At that time everything was still uncertain.

LAITH So I went by myself. But the marines here at the hotel told me to go to the Assassins' Gate in the Green Zone. At that time I didn't even know these words, Assassins' Gate, Green Zone. These were American words. I went there and it was really crazy.

SCENE TWO

The Assassins' Gate, an entry point into the Green Zone. Iraqis—a dazed-looking OLD MAN *in a tattered jacket, a pushy* WOMAN *in a black abaya—are standing in line, crowding forward, waving pieces of paper, speaking in Arabic and trying to get the attention of an American* SOLDIER, *who is trying to control the chaos. The* SOLDIER *is hassled but not hostile.* LAITH *takes his place at the end of the line.*

SOLDIER Hey, one at a time, one at a time!

WOMAN Mister, mister, please. (*She thrusts a piece of paper into his hand and says something in Arabic.*)

SOLDIER (*Trying to read—he's holding it upside down and she turns it over for him.*) What is this?

WOMAN Ambassador Braymer, Braymer.

SOLDIER What about him?

WOMAN Ambassador Braymer.

SOLDIER Do you have an appointment?

WOMAN Mister, please!

SOLDIER (*Gently moving her aside and pointing to the* OLD MAN) What are you here for?

The OLD MAN *speaks for ten seconds in Arabic, also clutching a sheet of paper. In the middle of it he begins to cry.*

English, dude, just give me a little English. Come on, don't cry.

OLD MAN No English.

SOLDIER I don't know what to tell you, man.

LAITH He wants to find out what happened to his four sons. They disappeared during Saddam's time. Their names are on this paper.

SOLDIER Dude! Where'd you learn how to talk like that?

LAITH Listening to American music. On VOA.

SOLDIER Cool. Like, what?

LAITH Mostly Metallica. "Draggin' me down, why you around?"

SOLDIER Get the fuck out of here! (*Calling to someone offstage*) Hey, Sergeant, this freaking Iraqi learned English from Metallica!

WOMAN Mister, please! Ambassador Braymer!

SOLDIER What does she want?

LAITH She has a petition for Bremer. She wants electricity, water, a job for her son, and she wants American soldiers to arrest the criminal gangs in her neighborhood.

SOLDIER Yeah, sure. Do I look like Superman?

LAITH No, the Incredible Hulk.

SOLDIER (*Takes the piece of paper from the* WOMAN, *puts it in his pocket, and pats her on the shoulder. She recoils slightly.*) Okay, calm down. I'll try to get this to Bremer. He's a busy guy.

WOMAN Thank you, mister.

SOLDIER Don't expect much.

LAITH *speaks to the* WOMAN, *who clearly doesn't take it in as she leaves.*

And I can't help this guy. Anything that happened during Saddam I got nothing to do with.

LAITH I know an organization that can help him. (*He speaks to the* OLD MAN *in Arabic, touching him reassuringly. The* OLD MAN *drops his head, wipes his eyes, nods, and shuffles off, still in a daze.*)

Sir, do you think I could get a job in the palace?

SOLDIER The palace is for pussies and bureaucrats, dude.
Come work with my unit, Alpha Company, the
Assassins. It'd be awesome. We do patrols, raids,
checkpoints. We definitely could use some interpreters.
What's your name?

LAITH Abdel-Aziz.

SOLDIER Whoa! Way too hard. Okay if I call you Al?

LAITH Sure. What's your name?

SOLDIER Jason.

LAITH Okay if I call you Jassim?

*They laugh and, after a moment, shake hands. It's a
first for both of them and they realize it.*

Just for your information, in Iraq it is considered rude
to touch a woman who is not your relative.

SOLDIER No shit. This is going to be a lot of fun.

LAITH We do every bad thing just like you, but in secret.
I'm sure it's different where you come from.

SOLDIER Actually, Muncie, Indiana, ain't a whole lot of
fun either. Guess that's why I'm here. Ever visited
America— (*He stops himself.*)

LAITH Never left Iraq.

SOLDIER Saddam was a motherfucker, wasn't he? (*Calling offstage again*) Hey, Sergeant, I think I just hired us a new terp. He's the shit! Name is Al and he's into metal!

LAITH *turns to the interviewer.*

LAITH So I became a terp with Alpha Company—the Assassins. To be honest, I sort of enjoyed it. I translated documents, I interpreted during interrogations, I went with them on raids. They treated me like a friend. But they didn't listen. That was a problem. I gave them information about insurgents, places where they kept weapons. I gave them an idea to buy back AKs and RPGs. But they never listened. I didn't know why.

Even before it got dangerous, I decided to keep my job a secret. I told my family and Adnan—that's it. This wasn't what I imagined before the war. I wanted to work for Apple or Microsoft or something. But it was a job. I got to improve my English. And I learned some things about Americans.

SCENE THREE

*The Assassins' Gate. Night: a spotlight casts long shad-
ows across the stage. From time to time there is the noise
of Humvees and distant gunfire.* LAITH *is leaning against
a wall with the* SOLDIER, *shooting the shit.*

SOLDIER So, like, you guys never do it before you get
married?

LAITH Didn't they give you some information before you
came here, sir?

SOLDIER Nobody told us a goddamn thing. I should
have been back in Muncie by now.

LAITH In our tradition we are supposed to be virgins
when we marry. Naturally, some Iraqis do not qualify.
Me, for example.

SOLDIER Dirty bastard—so why won't you introduce me
to your sister?

LAITH Of course there must be a double standard.

SOLDIER What happens to a girl if she messes up?

LAITH You mean (*he is wisecracking*) if she "brings
shame to her family"? And her brothers find out? (*He

19

draws his finger across his throat.) She gets whacked. The shame must be "washed," and then rinsed and dried.

SOLDIER Damn.

LAITH There is a popular medical specialty in Iraq devoted to examining girls. This is where reconstructive surgery can be very useful.

SOLDIER Not to mention oral sex.

LAITH Exactly. You know Ayatollah Sistani? Go to his website, sistani.org. He has a fatwa there about other kinds of pleasure for unmarried Muslims. He is very broad-minded. And then the Shia have *zawaj mutea*, temporary marriage.

SOLDIER Divorce?

LAITH Not really. An imam can arrange a marriage between two people for a certain period of time. It can be as short as an hour. There is a contract, a dowry, everything.

SOLDIER Like going to a hooker. So the imam is sort of a pimp.

LAITH Well, it's a kind of mercy. The Shia don't want to have forbidden sex, so they have *zawaj mutea*. It makes it easier to live.

SOLDIER Hey, I'm glad you guys are a bunch of hypocrites. I want every Iraqi having sex all the time, man. These dudes planting IEDs and taking shots at us, what they need is a good fuck. I'm serious, man, your culture's dangerous.

An Iraqi MAN *in a dishdasha approaches, angry looking. The* SOLDIER *takes his rifle off his shoulder and holds it at the "low ready" position, pointed toward the* DISHDASHA MAN's *feet. The* DISHDASHA MAN *glares at him and speaks to* LAITH *in Arabic in harsh tones.*

LAITH His brother was arrested by Americans last week, sir. He went to all the prisons, even Abu Ghraib, but he can't find him. He says his brother didn't do anything, he's just an importer of bananas.

SOLDIER (*Crowding the* DISHDASHA MAN *so that they're practically eyeball to eyeball*) Bananas. That's just beautiful. So your brother didn't shoot that RPG at my patrol last week? Didn't try to blow up Captain Prior's vehicle? He didn't kill Specialist Hunter? (*The* DISHDASHA MAN *says something disrespectful in Arabic.*) Hey, asshole, Hunter was my buddy in Basic. (*The* DISHDASHA MAN *answers again in kind. The* SOLDIER *turns to* LAITH.) Ask him if he knows anything about it.

LAITH *translates the question. The answer is a surly shake of the head.*

SOLDIER No pussy? Can't get any? Are you fucking your donkey, you sorry asshole? (*They're glaring at each other.*) Translate that, Al.

LAITH *and the* DISHDASHA MAN *speak in Arabic,* LAITH *trying to soothe him, the* DISHDASHA MAN *growing more heated. Finally, the* DISHDASHA MAN *turns to leave, then looks back at* LAITH *and, pointing a finger, says something hateful.* LAITH *returns to his post looking shaken.*

What'd he say? (LAITH *shrugs.*) Come on, Al, it looked like he just called your mother a whore.

LAITH He said, "Why do you work as an agent of the occupier? There is no safe place for traitors in Iraq."

SOLDIER Did he threaten you? Because I will personally break his fucking head if he ever messes with you.

LAITH Sir, this is a problem for us. The Baathists are making people believe that Iraqis like me are traitors; we are giving up Iraqis with false information and women are getting raped. Americans must put their message on television in a way that Iraqis can understand. Iraqi people listen to the Baathists in their neighborhoods, they hear al-Jazeera and Iranian television, and so they think you are stealing the resources. But they hear nothing from Americans, they get nothing from Americans. This is very dangerous for you and me.

SOLDIER Way above my pay grade, Al. Hey, your shift ended fifteen minutes ago.

LAITH (*Hesitating to mention this as he gets up to go*) Sir, there is a problem maybe you can fix. This light (*he gestures to the spotlight on top of the Assassins' Gate*)—when I walk home my shadow shows from a very far distance. It's dangerous. Can you turn it off until I go one hundred meters?

SOLDIER (*Caught for a moment*) Don't worry about it, dude, you're on our team. A sniper's got you covered the whole way. Guy could shoot an apple off that blast wall.

LAITH That's great. Good night, sir. (*As he leaves, his shadow precedes him.*)

SOLDIER Night, Al. Be safe.

SCENE FOUR

The hotel room. ADNAN *and* LAITH *are sitting as before.*

LAITH A few nights later I met one of the snipers. I said, "Thanks for covering me." "What are you talking about?" "When I go out." He started laughing. It was just a story to trick me. I got freaked out. I started changing my route home or the time I went out. The soldiers didn't want to deal with it—it was just easier. What could I do? Quit? There were hundreds more behind me. I was naïve, I believed the Americans wouldn't lie to us. We were friends, yeah, but they didn't trust us. That was my first shock—nobody's looking out for you. You're on your own.

ADNAN's *phone rings. He answers and has a short conversation in Arabic. He is trying to calm someone down, laughing gently. He hangs up.*

ADNAN This is our friend Firas in Damascus.

LAITH He ran away from Baghdad last month.

ADNAN He just had this vision that I will be killed by end of this month. He wants me to come to Syria and live with him. He says we can live on pasta. I told him it's not the time for plans. The problem is my family—I'm the only one supporting them. They are simple people, and I am the firstborn. They would die without me.

You know, it was Firas who got me the job at the embassy. His mother, the one who was later killed, she was a secretary in one of the offices and she told me they were looking for English-speaking Iraqis. I went to the Green Zone for an interview, and the one who interviewed me was exactly Bill Prescott—the one you also interviewed.

SCENE FIVE

An office at the embassy. PRESCOTT, *a State Department official in a blazer and necktie—youthful, clean-cut, with an embassy badge draped around his neck—is sitting behind a desk.* ADNAN *sits across from him.*

PRESCOTT Do you have any relevant experience?

ADNAN Before the war I was selling books on Mutanabi Street, selling anything, just to get money for smoking, as we say. I was not using my education at all.

PRESCOTT Where's Mutanabi Street?

ADNAN It is a place in old Baghdad where people sell books on the ground.

PRESCOTT Old Baghdad . . . God, I'd love to go there. It sounds so . . . Ottoman. I'd need a two-Humvee escort and permission from the regional security officer.

ADNAN It is a pity the Americans don't see the real city. It is a beautiful city—or it was.

PRESCOTT So how do you think this experience would help you as an interpreter in the political section?

ADNAN You mean, petty selling? Not at all. This was

how I was wasting my life. When the war came, I told myself: Now I will start to live.

PRESCOTT So you see it as a liberation? Not an occupation? Because our polling shows a split in Iraqi public opinion.

ADNAN I see it as a chance. Only that. A chance for every Iraqi. My experience is the experience of all the Iraqis of my generation who looked into the future and saw nothing, only darkness. We were living in this great prison. I know what this did to people in their minds. You cannot be successful here unless you understand the mentality. Perhaps this is a way I can be of help to you. I have been Iraqi all my life—this is my relevant experience.

PRESCOTT You don't think freedom and democracy are universal?

ADNAN I am not nearly smart enough to answer this question. But I know that you need to spend years to understand Iraqis.

PRESCOTT Then I have a hell of a long way to go, because I've only been here two weeks. At least I was in Riyadh before this. (*He tries out a little Arabic on* ADNAN, *who pretends to be impressed and answers in kind.*)

ADNAN For example, Iraq is part urban (*he gestures to himself*) and part Bedouin. This is why Iraqis shout: we need to be heard in the desert. Military victory is easy. But what will be after? You must change yourself when you come to Iraq. And we too must change, to understand you, because we can't have life without a common language between us. You must pay, and I must pay also. (*Pause*—PRESCOTT *is taking all this in.*) And believe me, when you finally know them, Iraqis are all good and nice and simple.

PRESCOTT That's an illusion Americans share about ourselves, so we should get along fine. Look, this section does extremely important and sensitive work. We report to the ambassador, and we deal with leading Iraqi politicians. Our job is to build institutions of democracy that will still fit the Iraqi context after the last American soldier goes home.

ADNAN Does this mean . . .

PRESCOTT Congratulations.

ADNAN That's wonderful. (*He extends his hand across the desk.*)

PRESCOTT Dress code is jacket, tie optional. You'll need to pay a visit to the RSO on your way out. Just tell him the truth and you'll be fine. (ADNAN *gets up to leave.*) Oh, I forgot to ask—are you Sunni or Shia?

ADNAN Is this important?

PRESCOTT Just so I know where you're coming from.

ADNAN Mr. Prescott, there is a sign on my wall at home: "Be honest without the thought of heaven or hell." This is where I'm coming from.

PRESCOTT I hope I haven't offended you.

ADNAN No. Only this is not a question we are used to being asked. You can't guess from my name? (PRESCOTT, *embarrassed, shakes his head.*) I am Sunni. We live in western Baghdad.

PRESCOTT That surprises me. I thought most Sunnis were against the Americans here.

ADNAN To be surprised is good. Many things in Iraq will surprise you. But I am not doing this job for the Americans.

PRESCOTT Why, then?

ADNAN For my country. And for myself.

On his way out of the office, ADNAN *runs into a young Iraqi woman on her way in. She is wearing slacks and a short-sleeved shirt, makeup, and no hijab. After a moment,* ADNAN *recognizes her.*

Intisar! What are you doing here?

INTISAR *looks perturbed to be seen and puts a finger to her lips to indicate: Don't tell. She sits down in the chair just vacated by* ADNAN *and her interview begins, though we don't hear it at first.* ADNAN *addresses the interviewer in front.*

We went to Baghdad University together in the nineties. Intisar was in my English literature class. She was a shy girl, very studious. She loved Emily Brontë. I remember once Saddam visited our college and Intisar pretended to be sick that day. We were never close friends, but there was something in the way she looked at me with those big unhappy eyes—I felt like she was my sister. She was another non-belonger.

SCENE SIX

ADNAN *goes into an adjacent office, where the* RE-
GIONAL SECURITY OFFICER, *a civilian in khakis and a
polo shirt, with an automatic pistol on his hip, hooks
him up to the lie detector machine. The* RSO *is all business. The polygraph exam takes place simultaneously
with* INTISAR's *interview.*

RSO Ever done one of these before?

ADNAN I saw it in a movie.

RSO Polygraph measures anxiety. The only thing to be
anxious about is lying. No lying, no problem. Put your
hands here and your feet here. That's good. Just relax,
take a breath. Don't close your eyes. Try not to move or
swallow. What did you have for breakfast?

ADNAN Tea and bread. (*Remembering, adding quickly*)
And yogurt.

RSO Have you ever lied to your parents?

ADNAN Of course. Who hasn't lied to his parents?

RSO Just yes or no. Have you ever had sex with a male?

ADNAN *stares at him.*

PRESCOTT Have you ever worked with foreigners before?

INTISAR There was no possibility of working with foreigners under Saddam.

PRESCOTT Do you think you'll have trouble adjusting?

INTISAR Adjusting to what?

PRESCOTT Well, I mean, our mentality (*he is borrowing from* ADNAN) can be a little different. Especially regarding women. I mean, compared to the Arab world.

ADNAN When I was younger. This is something normal.

INTISAR Mr. Prescott, do you know what my dream was as a girl? To ride a bicycle through the streets of Baghdad like my brothers. This is still my dream. It's a small dream. But if a girl did this, she would be looked at like a crazy person. Or a militia might shoot her while she is pedaling.

PRESCOTT They might shoot you for not wearing the hijab. We've had a few cases.

RSO Have you ever been involved in a plot on the life of any Americans in Iraq?

ADNAN Never.

RSO Ever had contact with insurgents of any kind?

ADNAN They live on my street, but I do not talk to them.

RSO Is that a yes or a no?

INTISAR It's true, they might.

PRESCOTT But you don't wear it. Even in your neighborhood?

INTISAR No. And there are people on my street who look at me with hate in their eyes. One of them said, "This is our area and our rules must be followed." I don't care. I don't care anymore.

PRESCOTT I'm curious—why not?

INTISAR I don't want to do anything that someone obliges me to do. I hate that. I won't do it. I was forced to do many things in Saddam's regime. I don't want to do that anymore.

PRESCOTT That's pretty brave of you, Intisar.

ADNAN There is no simple yes or no to this question. It is a gray area.

RSO This machine doesn't do gray areas. I need a simple yes or no.

ADNAN Every Iraqi knows someone who knows someone. But I avoid them. If they knew I was talking to you like this, they would kill me.

INTISAR It is not because I am brave. It is because I am hopeless.

SCENE SEVEN

The hotel room. ADNAN *is sitting as before with* LAITH.

ADNAN I thought I lost the job then. But at that time, before things got really bad, the polygraph was not so difficult, not like now. A week later they called me for the security briefing.

LAITH When I heard this news I was so jealous, I wanted to kill you! It was my dream to go into an important office every day, to wear a jacket and tie. And at that time my job with the Assassins wasn't good. Don't get me wrong, I liked the job. It was always something new. And the guys, they were very easy to know, very cool. But they did things—like, they never gave me the good body armor when we went on a raid, just some cheap vest that doesn't protect you against an AK. Or they took me out on patrol in my own neighborhood, even after I told them it was dangerous for me. I started wearing a bandanna over my face. We were losing our trust with the Americans and the Iraqis. The Iraqis stopped trusting you, and the Americans didn't trust you from the beginning. You became a person in between.

And then, interpreters I knew started getting killed. Like, five of my friends working in other units were killed. So I decided to quit, even though there were no other jobs.

ADNAN I told you to apply at the embassy.

LAITH I put on my jacket and tie and went to the Green Zone.

ADNAN And because you dress and talk like an American, you got the job. (LAITH *can't help clenching his fist in triumph at the memory.*) And you will never be able to pay me for this. I own your life.

LAITH I thought you were going to say because I'm Shia. (*To interviewer*) Actually, I didn't tell you this, but I'm a Kurdish Shia, a Feli Kurd. Maybe you've heard about us? We have a small community next to Sadr City. If someone asks am I Kurdish or Shia I say yes.

ADNAN And we thought all our dreams were coming true.

SCENE EIGHT

The embassy. The RSO *is at a podium giving the security briefing, with a PowerPoint display flashing slides on the screen behind him. Seated and facing him are* ADNAN, LAITH *(wearing a tie as well as a jacket),* INTISAR, *and* PRESCOTT.

RSO These security procedures could save your life or someone else's, so listen carefully. For those of you who are new: there are twelve checkpoints around the Green Zone. Americans with blue DOD badges can enter through any of them. Iraqis with yellow badges can enter here, here, and here after at least one and possibly several body searches and ID checks. These parts of the embassy that you see highlighted in red are classified and off-limits to anyone without DOD clearance. In case of mortar fire or other attack, an alarm will sound and you will evacuate to this rally point near the DFAC, then proceed in an orderly fashion into this underground bunker. Gas masks will be distributed along with hypodermic needles for self-injecting antitoxins. Do not leave your computer unsecured. Always log off before leaving your desk, even for a few seconds. The cell phone and badge you will receive after this briefing are your most important security items and I suggest you always keep them on your person. If you go into the Red Zone, make it a policy not to trust anyone you meet even if you think you know them.

Anyone coming in here from the Red Zone should be treated as a potential threat.

ADNAN, LAITH, *and* INTISAR *look at one another.*

PRESCOTT I don't think he means you.

RSO As you probably know, there've been some incidents recently, the suicide-vest bomber at the Green Zone Café, last week's indirect fire incident at the embassy annex. The enemy is trying every day and every way to penetrate the Green Zone perimeter, and he only has to succeed once. It's all about security. Questions?

INTISAR What is the Red Zone?

RSO The Red Zone . . . it's what's outside the Green Zone.

INTISAR You mean—Iraq?

RSO Congratulations and welcome to the American mission in Baghdad.

They all applaud themselves and one another. The RSO *distributes cell phones and badges, which the Iraqis drape around their necks with a touch of awe. Then* PRESCOTT *lines up* ADNAN, LAITH, *and* INTISAR *for a photograph. They are beaming.*

ADNAN *steps forward to address the interviewer.*

ADNAN To be honest with you, I didn't care if the RSO thought we were a potential threat. I loved my job. I loved having my official e-mail account and my voice mail. I loved going out with Bill Prescott to meet the head of this mosque or that political party, and then I loved writing up reports about these meetings, which even some people in Washington wanted to read. I even loved this badge, which became such a problem later. It said that I belonged to something, something very big. Before the war I didn't really try very hard in anything, just keep a low profile and get by. But when I started the job, the first thing I learned about myself was that I can make things happen. I would run here and there, I would kill myself, I would focus on one thing and not stop until I do it. That was the time I stopped waiting to live and started living. And for this, even though Bill Prescott had his weaknesses, I will always thank him.

SCENE NINE

The embassy. PRESCOTT *is sitting at his desk, with one eye on a television screen showing nonstop news from Iraq and Washington. Gradually the sound of the TV fades out, but the screen remains on.*

PRESCOTT Can we do this on background? I'm not really cleared to talk to you, but I'd like to be helpful because I think we don't always get our message out very well and the media sometimes misunderstands what we're trying to do. You asked why I volunteered to serve here. Look, just FYI: I'm from Springfield, Missouri, my dad has a small law practice, I went to Wash U, and I entered the foreign service after 9/11 for all the usual mom-and-apple-pie reasons. I believe in American exceptionalism—within limits. Not blindly. I knew we'd make a thousand mistakes in Iraq, but I also knew we were not here for oil or Halliburton. The Middle East is my generation's Europe and I wanted to be part of the effort to change the region. And by the way, that's a matter of national security as well as democratic values. I think it's a pile of bull crap to say that Arabs and Muslims don't want the same things we want. People are people, and every day in this job I see how much Iraqis deserve the chance to have a normal life. Do I wish the political process went faster? Yes. Do I worry about Sunni buy-in? Yes. But whatever you think about how we got here, it is what it is. Failure is definitely not an option. And we're making progress every day.

What I really want is for you to speak with one of the Iraqis on my staff. She's an extraordinary person, with more courage in her pinkie than most of us show over a lifetime. Her name is Intisar. I'm sure she won't mind speaking on the record.

INTISAR *enters the office and sits down nervously. She is dressed more conservatively than before, in a long-sleeved shirt.* PRESCOTT *steps out.*

INTISAR Well, you can quote me but don't print my name. Why? Because it isn't safe, they will kill me! You see this (*gestures to her long-sleeved shirt*)? Normally I don't like to dress like this, not in the summer in Baghdad. But I don't want them to notice me, especially because I won't wear hijab. I keep my makeup and perfume in my desk (*displaying them*) and wash off before I go home. If you are a girl coming at the checkpoint, you have so many things to fear, you cannot imagine. The general idea that other Iraqi people have about women who work in the Green Zone is, I'm sorry for the word, she's bitch. She's there to entertain Americans. There are some girls who did that, we have pictures they sent us by e-mail. I come from an open-minded family, that's why I'm working here, but that doesn't mean I am going to do something bad. So when I'm waiting in line—you know, those lines can take one hour or more, it's very dangerous—I hear men say nasty things about me. And these men are waiting in the same line!

You see these (*gestures to the badges around her neck*)? This one is for the Green Zone and this one is for the embassy. To Americans I am nobody without them, but to Iraqis they are like a target on my neck. When I come to work I keep this one in my shoe and this one someplace else (*laughs*). Last night there was some shooting in our street—we live in an insurgent area—and I woke up like: Okay, they're going to come, they're going to kill me and my family if they find the badges. Where can I hide them? So I put them in my closet, one in one pants pocket and one in a different pair. Yes, they know—my mom, my sister and brothers all know about my job—but I never tell them these things because I don't want them to be worried. Even in the morning when I go out from my house, we're thinking that maybe I'm not coming back. Lately my family is begging me to stop. But this is our only salary since my father died, and it is for my career.

The last few weeks I am taking medicine for stomach trouble. It's something unbelievable to be a target every day, to be wanted, and you just have a feeling that people are looking for you and you're on the street in the middle of them, you are not hiding. It is crazy.

Bill Prescott? He is a very nice man, but no, he doesn't understand all these things. He encourages us, he says be patient, things will get better soon. But Americans cannot have the feeling what it is to take these risks. They cannot understand.

PRESCOTT *reenters the room.*

PRESCOTT Finished? We've got an eleven o'clock at the parliament. (*To interviewer*) Isn't she something?

SCENE TEN

The Assassins' Gate. There are many more features of heightened security, such as coils of wire and red-lettered signs in English and Arabic with a variety of warnings, including "Cell phone use is prohibited at the check-point." ADNAN *and* LAITH *are standing in a line of Iraqis to get into the Green Zone. The* SOLDIER, *in full battle rattle, is checking badges—far more agitated and aggressive than earlier.*

SOLDIER Get back there! Yeah, you—don't cut my fucking line!

PRESCOTT *breezes past the line, holding up his badge.*

PRESCOTT (*To* ADNAN *and* LAITH) Hey, guys, how's it going? See you inside, I'm late for the ambassador.

SOLDIER (*Waving* PRESCOTT *on after a cursory check of his badge*) Go ahead, sir. (*To someone back in the line*) Hey, dickhead, I saw you cut! Get the fuck out of my line!

LAITH's *phone rings, a distinctive musical ring tone, perhaps the first bars of a Metallica song. He looks at it, hesitates, then answers in Arabic. After listening for a few seconds he abruptly hangs up, frightened.*

ADNAN Who was it?

LAITH *Alaas.* I don't know how he got this number!

ADNAN The brother of the banana importer?

LAITH You should have heard him.

ADNAN Then why do you use this phone outside the embassy?

LAITH "I'm watching you right now. You're wearing a striped shirt. You and your fat friend are agents and spies of the slaves of the cross. This is your second warning." Shit, I'm dead.

ADNAN Maybe it isn't serious.

LAITH I'm going to call Bill. I can't go to work today.

ADNAN That's what they want!

LAITH *begins to dial* PRESCOTT's *number. The* SOLDIER *sees him.*

SOLDIER Hey, dickhead! What does it say right there in two fucking languages? (*He shoves* LAITH, *grabs his phone, and begins to disassemble it.*)

LAITH Sir, that's an embassy phone! I'm an FSN! I have a yellow badge!

At the same moment, the SOLDIER *and* LAITH *recognize each other. There is a stunned silence between them.*

SOLDIER Al! What the fuck!

LAITH Jason.

SOLDIER What are you doing here?

LAITH I work here.

SOLDIER I didn't recognize you. Don't do that again, okay? I was about to bust your head open.

As he returns the phone there is a tremendous explosion not far away, followed by shooting and people shouting. Everyone ducks as the scene goes black.

SCENE ELEVEN

The embassy office. ADNAN, LAITH, *and* INTISAR *are at their desks.* PRESCOTT *is sitting on the edge of a desk.*

PRESCOTT I don't think there's anything we can do about it, guys. RSO controls security and badging.

ADNAN Can you speak to the ambassador?

PRESCOTT You expect me to go in and lay this on his desk? It's way below the ambassador's level.

ADNAN If you change our badge to green, we can avoid the line and do the search inside the gate.

PRESCOTT Let me get back to you. I'm not promising anything.

ADNAN We're getting threats.

PRESCOTT All of you? Intisar?

INTISAR Every look is a threat.

PRESCOTT Oh, a look . . . anyway, it can't be every look. Our polling shows forty-five percent of Iraqis support the interim government, which is an American ally.

ADNAN You always talk to the wrong people.

PRESCOTT (*Shooting him a look*) What's that supposed to mean?

INTISAR They all hate us. Sunni, Shia, it doesn't matter.

PRESCOTT I don't believe you. They don't all hate you. They don't all hate us.

INTISAR It's different. We are "traitors." Okay, I will tell you what happened. Last night I was walking from the taxi to my house after work. There is a man who is always on the street, selling cigarettes. His name is Abu Abbas. The children on the street call him Eggplant Face. He always said hello to me, until last week. Then he stopped. I didn't know why.

INTISAR *gets up from her desk and moves toward the shadows. Suddenly a man steps out and blocks her path.*

EGGPLANT FACE Intisar, where have you been?

INTISAR (*Startled, slightly frightened*) At work, of course.

EGGPLANT FACE Strange, a woman has a job when so many men can't find one. Where do you work?

INTISAR (*Thinking on her feet*) I'm a reservationist at

Royal Jordanian Airways. Do you want to book a ticket
to Amman?

EGGPLANT FACE Intisar, Allah knows when we lie.

INTISAR And he knows when we speak the truth. (*She
tries to walk on, but he blocks her way.*)

EGGPLANT FACE They say you work with Americans.

INTISAR Who says?

EGGPLANT FACE The brothers. They say this is why you
don't cover yourself.

INTISAR (*Quoting the Koran*) "In religion there is no
force." If I wear hijab it should be for Allah, not the
brothers or anyone else.

EGGPLANT FACE There are rules here. The defenders of
this area will not allow a woman to look like a
prostitute.

INTISAR (*Indignant, pushing past him*) You're the one
who thinks impure thoughts. (*She moves on and begins
to narrate again.*) I was really frightened. My mother
saw my face and asked what happened. When I told
her, she cried and said, "I won't allow you to leave the
house without hijab." This morning I wanted to know
how it felt. (*She stands before a mirror and picks up a
scarf. Hesitantly, she ties it around her head. She closes*

her eyes, tears it off, then puts it on again.) I hated it. In my family the boys and girls were treated equal. My father was always proud of his daughters. He told me once, "Your brothers don't cover their hair, why should you?" But I'll do it for my family. Because of my work I'll do everything the extremists want outside in the street, just to keep myself and my family safe from this *alaas*.

INTISAR *has returned to her desk, removing the scarf and putting it away.*

PRESCOTT So wear the hijab, then these *alaasa* will leave you alone. You're right, it's not worth it.

INTISAR But I feel like they have defeated me.

ADNAN What about the badges?

PRESCOTT (*Irritated*) I'll get back to you. And I know it's hard, but I really do need you guys here at eight a.m. (*Seeing the TV*) Hey, Secretary Rice is talking about the elections.

The office goes dark. The lights come up on ADNAN *and* LAITH *in the hotel room.*

ADNAN We didn't hear again about the badges. It was the kind of yes/no answer we became used to.

LAITH Believe me, this is worse than hearing no.

ADNAN Bill wanted to be our friend, but he had his own career, his own boss, the ambassador, and he didn't want to create problems. So he said yes/no. And the job continued, the lines at the Green Zone gate continued, the car bombs continued, the militias continued.

While ADNAN *is talking, outside the hotel there is gunfire. At first he doesn't notice and keeps going, then realizes that the interviewer is startled.*

You heard that? Sorry. You are frightened? It's okay, really. It happens every time.

LAITH For us it's like the sound of the clock.

ADNAN It was getting worse every week, but at the embassy nothing was happening. To come to work in the morning and go home at night, it was like two different worlds. From the inside, we saw that the Americans did not have control. But at that time still I believed more in my cause. I would say I am working for a cause—so if I die for it, let it be. All Iraqis are fatalist—we believe that if it is time to die, then let it die, so what? We don't know about the pleasures of life so much, so death to us wouldn't mean that much. To leave a miserable life, it's not that much to die. For you as an American, you can go everywhere and you do things you like and money is not a problem for you. Life is beautiful for you! Not for an Iraqi who doesn't have electricity, who is under threat. So what's the big deal to die and leave all this?

SCENE TWELVE

The embassy office. ADNAN *and* LAITH *are sitting at their desks, on which the photo taken after the security briefing sits.* INTISAR's *chair is empty; her hijab is on her desk. For some time they work at their computers in silence, every now and then looking at each other, at the door, at the eternal TV showing images from Iraq.*

LAITH You heard what Moqtada said? (ADNAN *doesn't answer.* LAITH *quotes Moqtada in Arabic.*) Moqtada! Future president of Iraq! (*Still no answer.*) What time is it?

ADNAN Why ask me? Ask your watch.

LAITH Call her.

ADNAN I called her fifteen minutes ago. The phone is switched off.

LAITH I think her uncle died maybe. She's at the funeral.

ADNAN Stop talking. It's useless to talk.

More silent work. ADNAN *is unable to concentrate.* PRESCOTT *walks in looking grim.* ADNAN *and* LAITH *stare at him.*

PRESCOTT I'm sorry. It's bad news. (*Pause—they are waiting for it.*) Intisar was picked up on her way home last night. (LAITH *continues to stare, but* ADNAN *knows and puts his face in his hands.*) They drove her around Mansour and they shaved off her hair and then they shot her and dumped her on the street. (LAITH *groans;* ADNAN, *face in hands, is motionless.*) We believe she was still alive, because a taxi driver came and got her. It appears he was working with them because he drove all over Karkh until she bled to death in his backseat. The driver ran into an American checkpoint on Haifa Street and he's been detained. We think it was Ansar al-Sunna. I'm very sorry.

ADNAN *can't stifle a sob.*

LAITH Intisar is dead?

PRESCOTT (*He too is stricken, with a new awareness.*) I— (ADNAN *lifts up his face to look at* PRESCOTT.) The embassy is taking up a collection for her family. (*He touches her hijab.*) I don't know if she forgot it or what. (ADNAN *is still looking at him, waiting for something more.*) I'm going to get you guys in with the ambassador. I should have done that before. I—

PRESCOTT *waits as if to hear their verdict on him. He goes out.* ADNAN *and* LAITH *are in their private worlds of shock. Then, slowly, they return to their computers. There is nothing else to do.*

SCENE THIRTEEN

The AMBASSADOR's *office at the embassy. There is an American flag in the corner and portraits of Bush and Cheney on the wall.* PRESCOTT, ADNAN, *and* LAITH *are sitting in chairs. The* AMBASSADOR, *in a business suit, is middle-aged, friendly but distant.*

AMBASSADOR Gentlemen, I'm sorry that it took this tragic incident for me to meet you. We've raised twenty thousand dollars in private donations for the family. I want to tell you it means a lot to us that you're still coming to work after this. You are the eyes and ears of this embassy. We could not do our work without you.

ADNAN (*Impatient with these formalities*) Sir, we have a problem.

AMBASSADOR I'm at your service.

LAITH It's our badges, sir. For our security.

ADNAN We are sacrificing our lives and until now we have seen nothing.

AMBASSADOR If it's badges, I think the best thing would be for you to speak to the RSO about it.

PRESCOTT Ambassador, it's about upgrading their clearances to—

AMBASSADOR Here's the guy who's in charge of badges.

The RSO *comes in, with his Glock pistol and his handcuffs. He doesn't sit.*

RSO Sir?

PRESCOTT We're hoping you can change the color of their badges to green.

RSO (*Looking at the Iraqis*) Their clearance is yellow.

ADNAN We have to stand in line for hours with all the other Iraqis. We are open to threats, to car bombs, to the sun, to the rain.

RSO Mm-hmm.

PRESCOTT Green would get them in faster.

RSO But they are Iraqis.

ADNAN We work at the embassy, we come here every day. We are FSNs. We are easily identified—our colleague was killed.

RSO You live in the Red Zone, right? That means you're under continuous threat. Someone finds out where you work, they could force you to smuggle something in here. It's happened. That's why we have these procedures.

LAITH We are just asking—

RSO If I change your clearance, I have to change the badges of four hundred other Iraqis working at the embassy and USAID. Can't do that.

LAITH (*Becoming confrontational in a slightly cheeky way*) These are words, not reasons.

RSO Anyway, green means weapons permit: yes. That's another security problem for me.

LAITH That's easy.

RSO Think so, huh?

LAITH Change it to "no" on our badges.

RSO Can't do it.

LAITH Why not?

RSO (*Getting tough, annoyed*) Embassy security is my number one priority. I won't do anything to jeopardize it.

PRESCOTT What about *their* security?

RSO (*Shoots an unfriendly look at* PRESCOTT) No way I can upgrade yellow badges to green. Anything else, sir?

AMBASSADOR I believe that's it. Thank you, gentlemen. My door is always open.

As they all leave the office, LAITH *says something to* ADNAN *in Arabic and* ADNAN *laughs. The* RSO *picks up on it.*

RSO Want to share that with me?

LAITH Just something Iraqis say. Like a proverb.

RSO I'm interested in Iraqi proverbs. I'm collecting them.

LAITH "We're blowing in a punctured bag."

RSO That's a good one. I'll be sure to write it down.

PRESCOTT (*Ushering* ADNAN *and* LAITH *away from the* RSO) Okay, guys, let's leave it there. We're all on the same team.

The RSO *leaves.* PRESCOTT, ADNAN, *and* LAITH *are standing facing one another.* PRESCOTT *is stunned and shamed and has a hard time looking at them.*

I'm sorry.

ADNAN This is a word that I am beginning to hate. Almost as much as "security."

PRESCOTT I can't believe they won't even upgrade your clearances.

ADNAN Because we are Iraqis. Intisar was Iraqi.

PRESCOTT Let's be honest, a green badge wouldn't have saved her life.

ADNAN At least she would know someone here cared if she died. What does this RSO know about Intisar? Does he know that she loved Emily Brontë?

PRESCOTT (*After a pause*) Listen, do you have a car?

LAITH An old one, like a cancer patient.

PRESCOTT Is there someplace you can take me in Baghdad?

ADNAN What do you mean?

PRESCOTT Like that street where you sold books.

ADNAN Why do you want to go there?

PRESCOTT I just feel like . . . I need to get out of here. It's like a sensory-deprivation tank. I don't know what the hell is going on out there.

ADNAN You have your intel reports.

PRESCOTT Don't mess with me. The blind leading the blind.

ADNAN Mutanabi Street isn't safe for you. And it's a violation of security. What will the RSO say? You need two Humvees and a military escort.

PRESCOTT I'm not going to tell the RSO. I'm just talking about slipping out for a few hours. What about your neighborhood?

ADNAN No way.

PRESCOTT (*To* LAITH) Or yours?

LAITH No *way.*

PRESCOTT For God's sake! Is there anywhere in Baghdad that's safe?

The scene goes dark. LAITH *steps forward into the light.*

LAITH My uncle owns a restaurant in Karrada, across the Tigris from the Green Zone. At least, he used to until he got kidnapped and his family paid fifty thousand dollars ransom. Now he's a refugee in Amman. Anyway, it was the only place we could think to take Bill. We told my uncle he was a Norwegian humanitarian worker.

SCENE FOURTEEN

A restaurant. PRESCOTT, ADNAN, *and* LAITH *are sitting at a table with plates of chicken, rice, and other Middle Eastern delicacies; otherwise the restaurant is empty. Next to them are* shisha—*water pipes. Arabic music is playing quietly.*

PRESCOTT What was up with that gnarly checkpoint after the bridge?

LAITH That was Jaish al-Mahdi, the Mahdi Army.

PRESCOTT That was JAM? How do you know they weren't police? The uniforms looked real.

LAITH They were police. And JAM. Didn't you see the picture of Sadr? Day shift, night shift—good cop, bad cop.

PRESCOTT What did you tell them?

LAITH That you're my mentally defective friend from Kurdistan.

PRESCOTT Seriously? And they believed you?

LAITH They're not very smart. I said some nice words about Moqtada and that was enough.

ADNAN Also the car. They will not believe this is a car for a VIP or any kind of foreigner.

LAITH You know, Bill, sometimes when there's fighting in Sadr City, I sleep in my car in the embassy parking lot.

PRESCOTT Man, you sleep in that car? Why can't you just get a trailer for the night? Half of them are empty.

LAITH Ask the RSO. Embassy security.

PRESCOTT Fuck the RSO. So what other things do you guys have to do? Tell me everything. Don't spare me.

LAITH When I drive to work I have a fake phone, one I don't use. I hide my embassy phone under the seat with my badges.

ADNAN Once I was in a taxi and you called—do you remember? I answered in Arabic and closed the phone in case you called again. The driver said, "Why did you close the phone?" I told him to drop me off far from my house, and I looked back to see if he was watching me from a distance.

PRESCOTT So I shouldn't call?

ADNAN You can send an SMS. But we cannot speak English on the street.

PRESCOTT Badges and phones are supposed to be for your security.

LAITH They are, what do you call it? A double-edged sword. (*He's pleased with himself.*) Even ourselves, we have code names in our address books for everyone we know.

PRESCOTT Why?

LAITH To keep our contacts hidden from kidnappers.

PRESCOTT Jesus. What if they threatened you, or beat the crap out of you?

ADNAN This is what we really fear, Bill. There are so many names we could give. And in my neighborhood, al Qaeda is becoming very strong and bringing their strict rules.

PRESCOTT What rules? Give me details. What do they do to people?

ADNAN No jeans, no shorts, no ladies driving. They threaten you if you have a spare tire in your car because this means you do not trust in God's help. They killed a man who always sold ice next to the vegetable market—he was a very poor man, everyone in the neighborhood liked him—because they said there was no ice in the time of the Prophet. This is their religion.

PRESCOTT Why haven't I heard about this?

LAITH In my area JAM has total control. They stop cars in the street to look for their enemies. That's why I leave my jacket and tie at the embassy.

PRESCOTT You're no safer with JAM than al Qaeda.

LAITH Not at all.

PRESCOTT So we're losing the Shia too.

LAITH Bill, people in Sadr City were looking for any tangible project. At the embassy I hear numbers of budget, amounts of money, this sewer system is going to be repaired, such and such schools are being rebuilt. But in the streets in my area there is not a tangible project.

PRESCOTT (*Ironically*) Are you suggesting our reconstruction trend lines are overly optimistic? Don't take that away, man, you're leaving me with nothing! Hey, it's dangerous hanging out with you guys. We go to a lot of expense and effort setting up mental blast walls and you're just blowing one big hole after another. You're a direct threat to embassy morale. RSO should investigate your ass.

ADNAN "Mental blast walls"—Bill, you are a great American. You seem like a different person than when we met.

PRESCOTT How did I seem then?

ADNAN You were—how can I say this?—almost like a

newborn baby. I didn't know such people existed in the world. This is what I love about America, and also it can make me crazy. For an Iraqi, to see such innocence, a part of us admires it. It makes us ashamed to think of our problems, our hatreds, as if we are carrying something unclean inside. And at the same time we want to take this innocence by the shoulders and shake it and shout, "Think! Look! Open your eyes! This is Iraq!"

PRESCOTT So what's my code name—Arabic for "retard"?

LAITH What is "retard"?

PRESCOTT Just a joke.

ADNAN Jokes are nice. We used to have so many jokes. Why don't you eat, Bill?

PRESCOTT Thanks, I'm really full. Where the hell is everybody?

LAITH My uncle told his customers the restaurant is having repairs.

PRESCOTT And the staff?

ADNAN He gave them the night off.

PRESCOTT (*Quieter, reflective*) I shouldn't have asked you guys to bring me here.

GEORGE PACKER

ADNAN We thought about it. We decided it was worth it. For you and us.

LAITH I heard a joke last week.

PRESCOTT Well, for God's sake let's have it before we all kill ourselves.

LAITH An American soldier in Sadr City is about to shoot a JAM guy, and the JAM guy says, "No, please, in the name of Imam Hussein!" The American says, "Who is Imam Hussein?" "He is our Prophet's grandson, our great martyr." "Okay," the American says, "I'll let you go in the name of Imam Hussein." A week later this same American is sent to Fallujah, and an al Qaeda guy catches him there. The American thinks and says, "No, please, in the name of Imam Hussein!" The al Qaeda guy says, "What? American and Shia?" and he cuts the soldier's head off.

PRESCOTT Do most Iraqi jokes involve beheading?

ADNAN Most of them involve someone stupid from Fallujah. Like the man on his wedding night—

LAITH This one is definitely *haram*.

PRESCOTT Then we have to hear it.

ADNAN And he asks his new wife to suck it. "No, no," she says, "it's against Islam." "But we're married." "I can't, it's *haram*!" "Please!" "Okay," she says, "but

BETRAYED 65

only if you put honey on it first." The man from Fallujah says, "If I put honey on it, *I'm* sucking it!"

PRESCOTT You should collect them in a book. It would be a bestseller in America. (*He is thoughtful for a moment.*) Hey, what did you mean, "You talk to the wrong people"? That's what you said before Intisar was killed.

ADNAN (*Hesitating—does he want to get into it?*) Not you, Bill. All the Americans.

PRESCOTT Okay. What did you mean?

ADNAN You talk to these politicians in the Green Zone and they tell you what they think you want to hear, and you tell Washington what you think it wants to hear, and everybody is happy, and Iraqis die and die and die.

PRESCOTT They're your elected leaders.

ADNAN We don't know them. You brought them with you and they lie to you. They don't care about the simple Iraqi people. They only care about their interests.

PRESCOTT So we should be talking to who?

ADNAN Your enemies.

LAITH I have some contacts with JAM guys in Sadr City, important people in his organization.

PRESCOTT How do you know them? No, don't tell me.

LAITH We all know them. One was my classmate in high school. He was really into motorcycles. Now he has a beard and an AK.

PRESCOTT How would you approach them?

LAITH I can tell them I work for an NGO. With money for trash collection or something.

PRESCOTT And?

LAITH Slowly I can find out if they want to meet Americans.

PRESCOTT They refuse to talk to the occupiers.

LAITH Some of them want to. There are differences within them. But they need a channel.

PRESCOTT I agree, it's what we need to be doing. But please just be really careful. My God, you live double lives, don't you?

LAITH (*Holding his hand up like a pistol*) We are James Bond without the nice lady or the famous gadgets.

ADNAN Bill, why don't you eat more?

PRESCOTT You guys are trying to kill me!

ADNAN There are easier ways. We could sell you to the jihadis for one hundred thousand dollars.

PRESCOTT I know. (*Pause*) Why haven't you?

ADNAN Because you came with us anyway.

SCENE FIFTEEN

The hotel room.

ADNAN It's strange to look back at how my life was after Intisar got killed. My friends at work became the only friends I have. My entertainment was at work, my pleasure was at work, everything was at work. It became my life.

LAITH There was nobody I could trust except Adnan.

ADNAN And I trusted Laith. We didn't have a secret life when we were together. But when we went out, we had to lie. And I hate to lie even about such a thing. So I avoided some of my oldest friends.

The lights go out—a power failure. Now they are talking in darkness. Every sound becomes a little louder—gunfire outside, a car horn.

Sorry. It even happens in this hotel. Soon they'll start the generator.

LAITH You have to always be aware of the car behind you. When you want to park, you make sure that the car passes you. You're always afraid of a person staring at you in an abnormal way. There's always a word that will go through your bones, like if someone says, "How is your work?"

ADNAN You work with the Americans and you get a threat. This threat will mean you are dead both ways—continue working with the Americans or stop working with the Americans. It's a circle, and you stay in it because there is no way out. It is more like inside your mind, you know? This threat will paralyze you, you don't think logically, in the end you can't think at all and you will do nothing, just stay at home waiting for them to come. And now that you are making me look at my life from the outside—it's unbelievable! What I did, the way I lived! The threat was always there, but I never felt it or paid attention to it. Whenever I thought deeply and seriously about my situation, I would block it and just move on. Because there's always the possibility that things will go wrong.

When it happens to your family, it is one hundred times worse. I tasted this a few months after Intisar's accident, when my younger brother Ahmed was kidnapped.

ADNAN *gets up and goes to stand alone in a circle of light, surrounded by darkness, staring at the display on his cell phone, which is ringing.*

ADNAN Allo? Ahmed? Allo?

A stranger answers him in a chillingly calm voice-over, in Arabic: No, this isn't Ahmed.

ADNAN *looks at the display to see if it's Ahmed's number calling and then continues in Arabic, his voice filling with terror as the situation becomes clear.*

ADNAN Who are you? Where is Ahmed?

Voice-over: Ahmed is here. I'm looking at him.

ADNAN Who are you?

Voice-over: He is tied up and he can't speak.

ADNAN Are you joking?

Voice-over: No. I'm not joking.

ADNAN I want to hear his voice, just let me hear his voice.

Voice-over: How do you want us to kill him? Shall we cut him into pieces and feed him to the dogs?

ADNAN No, no! Please don't hurt him, he's still a boy. Just tell me, tell me what you want.

Voice-over: Are you Sunni or Shia?

ADNAN Me? My family? We are—we are Shia.

Voice-over: Rejectionist infidels! You all deserve to die. Say goodbye to Ahmed.

There is a click.

ADNAN No! Please! Allo! Allo!

Frantically ADNAN *tries the number over and over and over—no luck. The phone rings again.*

ADNAN Sunni! We are Sunni! Don't hurt my brother. I told you Shia because I thought you were Mahdi Army. We are Sunni. I can prove it. Let me prove it.

Voice-over: Prove it.

ADNAN *returns to his chair in the darkness of the hotel room.*

ADNAN I made the wrong guess. They were Sunni extremists and I told them we are Shia. Fortunately, I have a friend who has connections with the insurgents in Amiriya and he explained the situation and they even apologized for the mistake and let my brother go. But before that, to me, the man said, "We are going to cut him into small pieces and feed him to dogs." (*The memory is still with him—he's staring at his phone.*) I will never forget that voice.

The lights come on again. LAITH *is patting* ADNAN *on the shoulder.*

LAITH The light at the end of the tunnel.

ADNAN You asked why didn't we quit? First of all, it's

not very easy to give up hope. Never. Always I hold on to the hope of things will get better, things will get better. This is what made all Iraqis live under Saddam. Second thing, the people I worked with, especially Bill Prescott—whenever we had problems like with the RSO, I saw Americans like Bill who understand me, who trust me, who believe me, who love me. This is what always kept my rage under control and kept my hope alive and kept me going. But now we're coming to the end of the story. (*To* LAITH) Tell him about the Sadr people.

LAITH Well, at first they were very happy to talk to me. I got a lot of important information about their activities, and Bill was so interested, and maybe in one or two more months I could arrange a meeting with him. But then Samarra happened—you know, the bombing of Askariya shrine. After that they stopped contact with me. JAM put all the effort now in killing.

ADNAN Political parties were encouraging the hate and telling the people this is your only chance now to survive.

LAITH My opinion, it started when the Americans came with Shia leaders and wanted to give the Shia leadership—

ADNAN And kick out the Sunnis. You admit this? Because you were not admitting it before.

LAITH They didn't want to kick out the Sunnis, but they

wanted to give Shia the power because most of the
Iraqis are Shia.

ADNAN And you believe the Sunnis did not want to
participate, right? My point is they didn't give them the
chance to participate. (*To interviewer*) This is one of the
things that we fight on.

LAITH In the first election the Shia parties were
encouraging Sunni parties to get involved in the election
and they didn't. And this was a mistake.

ADNAN The Sunnis didn't have the guarantees that the
Shia are willing to share the power. It's not because I'm
a Sunni, you know I don't care about Sunni and Shia—

LAITH Whatever.

ADNAN But I think the Shia made the Sunnis feel they're
against them.

LAITH No, no. The problem is the Sunnis think they are
the majority and the Americans try to tell them, no you
are not, the Shia are the majority. You have to share.
But they feel that no, we are the majority and we don't
support sharing, we want to have it for ourselves. So
they felt at the beginning anger against Shia because
they are now having the leadership, and this anger grew
to hate. Till now some of them can't accept that.

ADNAN The point is, it doesn't matter who started it. If
they want to reconcile and have a new start, they

should put everything behind and have this new start.
Everybody—the Sunni and the Shia.

LAITH I agree, this is not the point to think about, who
started it—now everybody is getting killed, the Shia and
the Sunnis. But if we think who started it, I think the
Sunnis started it.

ADNAN I think the Shia.

LAITH How is that? When is that?

ADNAN I told you, when they came here they kicked
every Sunni out.

LAITH They kicked themselves.

ADNAN No. I met a lot of Sunnis who were willing to
participate and they couldn't, they were prevented.

LAITH I didn't see that.

They are looking hard at each other.

ADNAN (*In Arabic*) Death to rejectionists! Long live the
Islamic State of Iraq!

LAITH (*In Arabic*) Our blood and souls we sacrifice to
you, oh Moqtada! *Nam, nam*, Moqtada!

Both of them burst out laughing.

ADNAN We are arguing for the past two years. But when I feel that I'm pushing too much and he starts to become so angry, I pull the brake. And now, really, there is no more reason to argue because everything is ending.

LAITH (*Quietly*) That's true.

ADNAN You have to tell him.

LAITH Well, it's so funny. Because with all the threats and dangers, you will never expect where the biggest one is going to come from.

SCENE SIXTEEN

The embassy office. ADNAN *and* LAITH *are working. The* RSO *comes into the room and stands silently over* LAITH'*s desk.* LAITH *looks up, startled.*

RSO I need to see you.

LAITH (*Exchanging an apprehensive look with* ADNAN) Why?

RSO Just something work related.

LAITH Actually I'm busy. I'm writing a memo for the political counselor. What about tomorrow?

RSO Uh-uh. Now.

ADNAN You don't have to go. Remember what happened to Ameer and Riyadh.

RSO If you didn't do anything wrong, nothing's going to happen.

ADNAN Ameer and Riyadh didn't do anything except they made some small mistake on the polygraph. They were fired and Riyadh stayed three weeks in Abu Ghraib.

RSO Let's go.

LAITH I want to tell my supervisor. (*To* ADNAN) Where's Bill?

ADNAN At parliament. I'm calling him now.

As LAITH *goes out with the* RSO, ADNAN *picks up his cell phone and calls.*

Bill, you have to come to the embassy as soon as possible.

SCENE SEVENTEEN

The RSO's *office.* LAITH *is seated before the polygraph machine, not yet hooked up.*

RSO   What are you so nervous about?

LAITH   I'm not nervous.

RSO   (*Laughing*) Why are you hyperventilating?

LAITH   What?

RSO   Breathing hard.

LAITH   I know what happens to FSNs you want to talk to about something work related.

RSO   What happens to them?

LAITH   They disappear.

RSO   Tell me about your work. What do you do?

LAITH   I'm an interpreter in the political section.

RSO   Tell me more.

LAITH   I go with Bill Prescott to meetings. I interpret

for him with Iraqi politicians. I write reports on Iraqi politics. I give information about the Arabic press.

RSO Are you Sunni or Shia?

LAITH *folds his arms across his chest and doesn't answer. The* RSO *takes his zip cuffs off his belt and lays them on the table.*

LAITH I'm a Feli Kurd.

RSO A what?

LAITH Kurdish Shia.

RSO Huh. (*He is momentarily stumped.*) Where do you live?

LAITH Sadr City.

RSO Are you a Sadr guy?

LAITH I'm an Iraqi.

RSO That's nice. I bet there's a proverb about it. So are you one of Sadr's guys?

LAITH No way.

RSO Do you get phone calls from Sadr's guys?

LAITH I'll be lucky if I get a phone call from Sadrists. My supervisor will be very happy.

RSO Why's that?

LAITH It's our work.

RSO Do you know what an EFP is?

LAITH Like the really big IEDs from Iran.

RSO Do you know how many Americans have been killed by EFPs? Do you know who's planting them?

LAITH Of course, the Shia militias, mostly Jaish al-Mahdi.

RSO And you're talking on the phone with these guys?

LAITH My supervisor gave me instructions.

RSO You know what? I'm really dissatisfied with this conversation. I don't feel I'm getting any cooperation from you at all.

LAITH I don't know what you want.

RSO No cooperation, just bullshit.

LAITH I'm telling you the truth.

RSO You're not a Sadr guy, but last week you wrote an

e-mail to the military liaison office asking about a detainee named Sami Abdel-Rahman. They forwarded it to me. (*The* RSO *looks triumphant.* LAITH *shrugs.*) Who told you to do that?

LAITH I was asked by one of my contacts in Sadr City.

RSO The same one that sent you here?

LAITH Sent me here?

RSO To work at the embassy.

LAITH No one sent me here. Bill Prescott knows my background. You gave me a lie detector.

RSO Yeah, you did better that time. Now you're not cooperating and it's starting to piss me off. So we're going to do it again.

LAITH Why now? The annual polygraph is in September.

RSO That's right, but you're choosing not to cooperate so I have to do a special one for you. Just sit still. (*The* RSO *begins to strap* LAITH *to the machine.*) Sit motionless. Don't close your eyes. Don't swallow. I said don't swallow. What's the name of your contact in Sadr City?

LAITH Hazem al-Khafaji.

RSO How do you know him?

LAITH From school.

RSO Did you ever conspire with him against the lives of American personnel in Iraq?

LAITH No, never.

RSO Why did you place seventeen calls to him between January and April?

LAITH Bill Prescott told me to open a channel.

RSO Did he tell you to send an e-mail to the military liaison office?

LAITH No.

RSO Asking about Sami Abdel-Rahman?

LAITH No.

RSO Do you know what Sami Abdel-Rahman is accused of?

LAITH I think he was caught when they did the sweep in Shaab.

RSO Planting EFPs on coalition patrol routes.

LAITH I didn't hear that.

RSO You're hearing it now. He has coalition blood on

his hands. Did you give Sami Abdel-Rahman
information about coalition patrol routes?

LAITH No!

RSO Are you lying to me? If I stop this test and report
the results to D.C., we'll see what happens to you.

LAITH How could I know the routes? I don't have
classified access.

RSO You're the guy who wanted the green badges,
right?

LAITH For our security.

RSO Green would have gotten you past the outer
checkpoint without a search.

LAITH Maybe it would have saved someone's life.

RSO That was the first red flag to me. Did you hear
Prescott or anyone in the embassy talking about patrol
routes?

LAITH Never.

RSO Why did you send the e-mail?

LAITH Because my contact asked me to do him a favor.

RSO You use your job here to do favors for the enemy.

LAITH It's a kind of courtesy, to show good faith. I sent the e-mail on my state.gov account and I know you can read them. I wasn't trying to hide.

RSO State.gov is for official business, correct?

LAITH Yes.

RSO Did you have official clearance to ask about the status of that detainee?

LAITH I'm telling you, it was part of my job. I was trying to keep the channel open.

RSO No official clearance.

LAITH Maybe I should have asked Bill.

RSO Did you ask about the status of any other detainees?

LAITH No. I mean, once, yes. The brother of my friend was brought in on a mistake.

RSO No? Yes? No? This machine is going off the charts.

LAITH Yes, for my friend.

RSO So you're using your official position to do favors for friends? Enemies, friends, doesn't matter just so long as they're Iraqi?

LAITH My friend was going to tell some people about my job.

RSO Your friend was?

LAITH Someone I know. He began to guess where I work and he was threatening to tell the JAM in his neighborhood. So I had to do this for him.

RSO You know what? The simpler the answer, the happier this machine. It doesn't like complicated answers. It doesn't trust them. Complicated answers means you aren't cooperating. It means you are fucking lying to me.

LAITH Every day, every day I'm risking my life for this embassy.

RSO You are trying to fuck with the United States.

Calmly, LAITH *removes the polygraph wires from his body, takes off his badge and phone, and places them on the table.*

What's this?

LAITH I'm resigning my position.

RSO You can't. You've been fired.

LAITH You can't fire me. The political counselor has to sign the order. I resign first.

RSO (*Snatching the zip cuffs*) You are not walking out of here on your own.

The RSO *ties* LAITH's *hands in zip cuffs and marches him out to the embassy office, where* PRESCOTT *and* ADNAN *are standing.* ADNAN *and* LAITH *embrace and speak quietly in Arabic while* PRESCOTT *and the* RSO *argue.*

PRESCOTT What the hell is this?

RSO You've got an enemy agent working in your office.

PRESCOTT What is this man doing in handcuffs?

RSO He failed the polygraph. He's a liar and a subversive. He's going to collect his possessions and be escorted out of the Green Zone.

PRESCOTT You have no authority to do this. I'm telling you to release him.

RSO You do your job and I'll do mine.

PRESCOTT You're making my job impossible.

RSO You should keep better track of your staff. Hey, don't touch his computer. (ADNAN, *rigid with anger, is putting* LAITH's *possessions—photographs, etc.—in his bag.*) And that phone stays here.

ADNAN It's his personal phone.

LAITH My decoy.

RSO It stays here.

PRESCOTT *snatches the phone from the* RSO *and drops it in* LAITH's *bag. They face off, staring each other down, while* ADNAN *unties and removes* LAITH's *necktie.* LAITH *holds up his hands to indicate that he can't remove his jacket with his hands cuffed.*

That isn't embassy property.

PRESCOTT He can't go out into the Red Zone wearing this. That's what makes him an "enemy agent." Do you get it? Do you get it at all?

The RSO *shrugs and releases* LAITH *from the cuffs so that he can take off his jacket and hand it to* ADNAN. *Immediately he is cuffed again.*

RSO Take your bag and let's go.

ADNAN All the sacrifices, all the work, all the devotion mean nothing to you. We are still terrorists in your eyes.

PRESCOTT I'm going to have you investigated for this. (*The* RSO *ignores him.*) You have no idea what this office does. You have no fucking idea what these men do for us. You're driving out the best.

RSO My advice? You're way overstressed. Take some R&R. A week in Dubai.

LAITH It's okay, Bill. I appreciate everything you did for me. You're a friend. (*As the* RSO *escorts him out*) But I think the U.S. is still in a war. I don't think you're going to win this war if you don't win the hearts of your allies.

As LAITH *and the* RSO *leave,* PRESCOTT *slams his fist on a desk.*

SCENE EIGHTEEN

The hotel room.

LAITH That was the first time I hated the Americans.

ADNAN You wouldn't talk to me for a week.

LAITH I went home and didn't see anybody. It was like somebody died and I was attending the funeral, but the body in the casket was mine. It was like my girlfriend threw me out of her life. Without my job I didn't know what to do. I fell in between heaven and hell. The Americans didn't want me and the Iraqis didn't want me. Where will I go? Help yourself by yourself, that's the best way. Find a solution for yourself. But I can't see any solution. I am, how do you say it, hung out to dry.

ADNAN Bill did go on vacation after that. Not to Dubai. He went home to Springfield, Missouri. We heard that something strange happened to him.

As ADNAN *continues,* PRESCOTT *acts out what is described. At some point* LAITH *slips out of the hotel room.*

Bill was sick somehow. Maybe he was overstressed. He was driving his car and maybe he dreamed he was in Iraq. His mind went black or something.

PRESCOTT Sniper! Watch out!

As PRESCOTT *swerves, there is the noise of a car skidding out of control.*

ADNAN And then he drove off the road. It was terrible. We heard he had three operations. Anyway, he never returned to Baghdad. I think he was like the soldiers in those movies about Vietnam. They go home and something has changed. They are not the same as before.

   That was a few weeks ago. I am still at the embassy, but everything is different. The woman who came to replace Bill is not the same. She is really not into the Iraqis. And without Intisar and Laith, I am working just to keep working, to do something. When I go outside I am very tense, I am on my toes watching around and being afraid. When I am inside the embassy I am tense, I am on my toes, watching around, afraid that I will be got. I tell myself, my turn is coming, my turn is coming.

LAITH (*Getting up from his seat and acting out what he describes*) Last week, I went outside my house to put fuel in the generator. I found a piece of paper lying by the door. It was in Arabic. It said, "We will cut off the heads and throw them in the garbage." Did it come from al Qaeda or Jaish al-Mahdi? There was no signature. I didn't take it for serious until I saw something next to the fence. (LAITH *discovers the severed upper half of a small dog. He picks it up and examines it, then reads the note again and looks around in terror.*)

ADNAN And then he knew it was serious. Maybe this was the final warning from the brother of the banana importer. They found his house. So he came to stay here at the hotel. (LAITH *returns to the hotel room and sits down beside his suitcase.*) He was most welcome at my house, but it's too dangerous for a Shia stranger on my street.

LAITH Anyway, in a few weeks he would be sick of me and kick me out. But I can't stay in Baghdad. They will find me sooner or later. Nowhere to run, nowhere to hide, you know?

ADNAN When I told him about you, he said, "Why do I need to talk to this person? Why take the risk?" I told him maybe you can help. Not like a quid pro quo, but just because you know the story now and maybe you understand our situation enough to do a small favor.

LAITH Anyway, how can a simple Iraqi in Baghdad find a telephone number in Springfield, Missouri?

ADNAN Try it again. Hurry up, it isn't safe for our friend to stay here much longer.

LAITH *dials the number. This time it goes through.*

LAITH *Al-hamdullilah.*

SCENE NINETEEN

PRESCOTT's *bedroom in Springfield.* PRESCOTT *is lying in bed with bandages on his face, hands, and arms. On his desk there is the picture of* ADNAN, LAITH, *and* INTI-SAR. *The phone on the desk rings. He can't or won't answer, so we hear an outgoing message say, "This is Bill and I am so totally fucked up that you'll have to leave a message," then* LAITH's *voice on the answering machine.*

LAITH (*Voice-over*) Bill, *habibi, shlonek?* (*More greetings in Arabic*) We miss you. We were so worried when you didn't come back. Did al Qaeda put a sleeper cell in Springfield, Missouri? (PRESCOTT *laughs painfully, then groans.*) Really, we are very worried. Call and tell us that everything is okay. Baghdad is going to hell without you. You will never guess—we are sitting in Palestine Hotel with that journalist who interviewed you and Intisar. We are telling everything, the good, the bad, and the ugly. We told all your secrets. Now you have to give your side of the story. Just kidding, *habibi.* We said you are the only American we trust. (*After a pause*) Bill, sorry, I have a little problem. It's a little urgent so please call me. Sorry to bother you.

ADNAN's *voice comes on.*

ADNAN (*Voice-over*) Bill, Laith has a very serious

situation. Last week he had a direct threat. If there is any way to get him out of Iraq . . .

LAITH's *voice resumes.*

LAITH (*Voice-over*) He is exaggerating, Bill. You know how Iraqis love to exaggerate. We miss you, that's it, we are waiting to hear. *Masalama, habibi, masalama.*

There is a click. PRESCOTT *lies motionless for a few seconds, taking it in. Then, with a groan of pain, he sits bolt upright.*

SCENE TWENTY

PRESCOTT's *bedroom. He is sitting at his desk, talking on the phone. Simultaneously,* ADNAN *and* LAITH *are seen in the hotel room, sharing one cell phone.*

PRESCOTT The ambassador's in D.C. for meetings. I'm going to try to get an appointment and fly out there.

LAITH How can you travel? You are totally fucked up.

PRESCOTT True.

LAITH But why will you meet the ambassador?

PRESCOTT To see about getting you a visa to the U.S.

LAITH They will never give me one.

PRESCOTT Maybe not. But it's worth a try. There's a case for it.

LAITH Anyway, what would I do with it? Go to the U.S. and do what?

PRESCOTT Ask for asylum.

LAITH Do you think they would give me an asylum in the U.S.? Never.

PRESCOTT Why never?

LAITH For the U.S. to give an asylum for an Iraqi, it means they have failed in Iraq.

PRESCOTT (*After a pause*) I'm the one who failed in Iraq.

LAITH No way, Bill.

PRESCOTT I can't go back. None of my projects got off the ground. I left you guys hanging. It's embarrassing—I wasn't even in combat—I don't really even know what happened to me. But I didn't achieve anything in Baghdad, that's for sure.

ADNAN *takes the phone from* LAITH.

ADNAN Bill, we totally appreciate what you are doing. But you know, there are so many Iraqis in this situation. Only a few of us are left at the embassy. All the others are hiding, or they went to Syria and Jordan, but our Arab brothers don't want us and we cannot live in those countries.

PRESCOTT I'm aware of it. Feel free to give your colleagues my e-mail. Seriously. Washington isn't doing anything.

SCENE TWENTY-ONE

PRESCOTT's *bedroom. He is reading his laptop screen, shaking his head, putting his hand to his forehead. One by one, a series of Iraqi* CORRESPONDENTS *take turns stepping into a spotlight.*

FIRST CORRESPONDENT Dear Mr. Prescott: The whole neighborhood cannot forget that I worked with U.S. Army sometime in the past and I feel that someday a close-minded neighbor will reflect his anger toward the U.S. troops on me, especially that they were seeing me inviting U.S. soldiers to come to my house, that is why I got diabetes since I quit working with the army, the matter that led me to have heart complications. Do you imagine that I was forced to dig a well in the yard of my house to get water for almost one month? I still keep in a hidden place some of the souvenirs I received from the soldiers, among them are photos which I took in 2003 for some of my friends in the battalion I worked with in which they hold my newly born daughter (she is now four years old) in their arms inside my house. Other souvenirs are recommendations, uniforms, caps, military sunglasses, ID cards. The above-mentioned prelude would not explain to you a small percentage of how I miss those days and how I am willing to leave Iraq forever and find a safer place for my family as I am living in a society that looks at me as a betrayer and should be outcasted. I tried before one month to join the program that helps translators to apply for immigration to the States but the time was not in my side and I needed to contact some of the officers I worked with but did not have their addresses. Sorry for making it so long but this is like a drop from the sea of sadness and frustration I am drowning at. Sincerely, Ayad Hamid

SECOND CORRESPONDENT Dear Sir: Since June 2004 I work for U.S. Regional Embassy Office in Hilla. My story is a long one and I have a lot to say but the hottest and burning issue is what is happening to me at the moment. Three weeks ago I received a threat from the Sadr militia and I tried to hide for some time but just a week ago my brother was kidnapped by a militia group belongs to the new elected democratic government of Iraq which is supported by the U.S. government and the President Bush. If I am lucky to receive my brother's body I will try to leave to Syria but I am lacking funds and the office will only give me one month leave, but this problem will take a long time and I cannot live without job. Please send me any advise. Sorry to bother you with my problems. Mwaffaq Salem

THIRD CORRESPONDENT Dear Mr. Bill Prescott: According to my friends in Baghdad, you are helping Iraqis to gain asylum in the U.S. Thank you for your efforts, you are aware of the suffering in Iraq. I worked for CPA in 2003 and KBR in 2004. I was forced to leave Iraq immediately after my husband was killed by mujahideen because of working for Americans. I live in Amman.

My refugee card from the UN is attached. I also attached some of my recommendations including from Mr. Bernard Kerik. Can you help me with asylum to America. Thank you very much. Best regards, Zina Qasim al-Tamimi

FOURTH CORRESPONDENT Hi Bill, I think you remember me, we had lunch in the DFAC after the elections last December 2005 and you told me about problems with your girlfriend and I told you the same. You will not imagine, everything ended for me right here in Cairo where I am now with nothing after the Egyptian authorities arrested two families which were with us trying to escape to Europe. The traffickers ran away with the documents and the money of the rest of the group which includes me, so I ran to some Iraqi friends who are living in Cairo and decided to hide me. I have nothing to lose. Before leaving Iraq I was diagnosed with brain cancer but I am not suffering from any painful symptoms till now, actually I am amazed of the survival instinct that makes me carry on and try to cherish further hope in life. Sorry to disturb you, I guess I like to talk a lot, as you know I always enjoyed it. As you can see now we have two totally different prospects. Take care. *Shukran ya wardah*, Bill. I know that not all Americans are the same, you are diverse in everything, even your moral values. I appreciate your help and I wish those who were more excited about the drums of the wars had the courage to deal with its consequences rather than to keep silent about the plight they left us in. *Allah yubarik feek*. Ibrahim

SCENE TWENTY-TWO

An office at the State Department in Washington. On the wall are pictures of Bush, Cheney, and Rice. PRESCOTT, in suit and tie, is sitting in front of a desk, the bandages now removed from his face, which shows scars. Behind the desk sits the AMBASSADOR, just the same as in Baghdad.

AMBASSADOR It's good to see you're recovering.

PRESCOTT I wish I could return to the mission.

AMBASSADOR Well, I'm coming back to Main State myself in a few weeks. There's only so much any of us can do at this point. It's more and more up to the Iraqis.

PRESCOTT Do you remember the Shia interpreter in my office?

AMBASSADOR I . . . don't really have a good memory `for . . .

PRESCOTT The one who asked about upgrading FSN badges to green, which never happened.

AMBASSADOR I . . . vaguely.

PRESCOTT The one who was fired.

AMBASSADOR Yes, right.

PRESCOTT He's in a serious jam and he needs to leave Iraq. Sir, I hope DOS will recognize his service and grant him a visa.

AMBASSADOR But he was fired.

PRESCOTT RSO overstepped the bounds. It was some kind of vendetta. He should have been counseled, not fired. He was acting on instructions and took it maybe a step too far, but he was a trustworthy, loyal employee.

AMBASSADOR If he failed a polygraph, there's a security risk. I don't think there's much chance he'd get past DHS even if we did clear him.

PRESCOTT Sir, if you made a case for it. He was a military interpreter before joining the embassy. He risked his life for the United States for three years.

AMBASSADOR I'll see what I can do, but I doubt it'll be much use.

PRESCOTT (*Producing a piece of paper from his jacket pocket*) Sir, in the past week I've been getting bombarded with e-mails from Iraqis who worked with us. The stories are incredible. There are eleven names on this list (*he places it on the* AMBASSADOR's *desk*) after one week of word of mouth getting around, with contact information and personal histories. Sir, these are all people who put their trust in us. Think how many drivers, interpreters, contractors, media fixers are in the same situation. There must be thousands.

AMBASSADOR It's terribly sad.

PRESCOTT A minute ago you said there's only so much we can do. I agree. But this is one thing we still can do.

AMBASSADOR What are you suggesting?

PRESCOTT Find out where they are. Get them out. Bring them here.

AMBASSADOR Bring thousands of Iraqis here?

PRESCOTT These are our friends.

AMBASSADOR A mass exodus from the Green Zone? What would be the optics of that? It would mean game over, we're on our way out.

PRESCOTT I agree we would need procedures so we don't encourage people to become refugees. But once they make the decision to leave, I believe, with all due respect, that we have an obligation.

AMBASSADOR An obligation based on what?

PRESCOTT Because we're Americans, sir. Do you remember what Ford said about letting in the

Vietnamese? "To do less would have added moral shame to humiliation." This is just the same.

AMBASSADOR Ah, but you see, that's the problem. You've uttered the magic word. It isn't just the same as Vietnam. I was there, you know, in seventy-five. I was about your age, a junior FSO. And in April seventy-five the situation was clear. The war was lost. In Iraq the president has declared his determination to win. How can we resettle large numbers of Iraqis here when we are still in the fight there?

PRESCOTT Do you think we can win, sir? What would winning mean?

AMBASSADOR My personal views are irrelevant. This is the president's policy, and you and I and everyone in this building are committed to carrying it out or else we should tender our resignations.

PRESCOTT (*Waving the sheet of paper*) What about them? Do we owe them anything?

AMBASSADOR (*Slowly, reflectively*) I believe . . . we owed Iraqis a shot at a better life. Yes, we most certainly broke it, and we owned it. And I believe . . . we gave them a chance—many, many chances—to express their desire for a free and democratic society. To build that better life. Most of them have showed that they don't share our vision, for all sorts of reasons, cultural, religious, nationalistic. Perhaps the vision was misguided from the start. That's for the historians to decide. But we could not impose it. We could only offer it.

PRESCOTT The people on this list share it. They risked everything for it. They're losing everything for it.

AMBASSADOR Bill, this is not something to push back on. You'll get the wrong kind of reputation. My view is you should focus on your recovery right now. And before coming back to the department, I advise you to give some thought as to whether the foreign service is the right path for you. It is certainly not for everyone.

PRESCOTT (*Getting up to leave*) I've already thought about it, sir. I wanted to see what you would say before I made a decision. But if no one will do anything about this from the inside (*he folds the piece of paper in his jacket*), then I'm going to try from the outside.

SCENE TWENTY-THREE

The hotel room. LAITH's *chair is empty, his suitcase gone;* ADNAN *is alone.*

ADNAN Laith was right. There was no U.S. visa for him. But Bill pulled a string in the Italian embassy in Baghdad, and Laith got a visa for the European Union. He flew to Rome and from there he took the train to Sweden, where all Iraqis try to go. Sweden—not even a member of the coalition of the willing.

I miss Laith. It's strange to still be here without him. (*Holding up his ring finger, with a string now tied around it*) Before he left he gave me this, so neither of us can ever forget. I miss Intisar too, and I miss Bill. Sometimes I feel I'm the last person in Baghdad. I resigned from the embassy one week ago. I gave the RSO my badges. It was so simple to quit! No photos, no party, that's it. And now I can leave Iraq anytime. Bill got the same visa for me that Laith got. I want to travel to the U.S. to see him and thank him, but they will not give me a visa either.

When I started working with the Americans it was like starting to live for the first time, and I threw myself into it. Now that life is over and I have to start a new life again somewhere. I am thirty-five. For an Iraqi this is very old.

ADNAN *gets up out of the chair and walks to another*

room, where there are piles of books, documents, photos, and an empty petrol can.

In the last two weeks I started a campaign of burning at my house. My attitude is always try to keep memories. For example, I kept the menu from Laith's uncle's restaurant the night we went there with Bill (*he holds it up*). And the picture we took when we got our jobs (*he does the same*). My books—here is *The Outsider*, about the non-belonger. But I'm trying to get rid of these things, to pack one bag as small as possible if I want to escape, so if insurgents come into the house they will not find anything.

He stuffs things in the petrol can and lights a match to it.

I have two more trash bags full of things to burn. I told my family these are old lectures from my college days I don't want anymore. It's lies! I have to burn a lot of things that really I am sad about. And I still have more things to burn. Since the garbage guys are starting to be killed I cannot put the bags on the street. The idea of burning is that you don't leave a track. I have this bad habit of keeping everything like memories. I don't know where I read somewhere, if you want to make a new start you need to put the closure, so this burning of things is like kind of closure. (*His voice is getting soft.*) I have my schedule for every week the entire life I worked at the embassy. My notes from meetings. History.

ADNAN *watches the papers burn down.*

The last months at the embassy, when I went home at night, the streets were nearly empty. I would find my mother sitting near the main door to our house, at the garden, waiting for me, praying and crying. I said, "My God, I am killing this woman. I have to stop." But I cannot just stop work and stay home, so I have to find another solution. Now the other solution just presented itself to me. I can leave any day. But I'm waiting, like I'm paralyzed between staying and going. I don't want to see the face of my mother and my father when I leave.

It is strange to think of becoming Swedish. I will have to be like a small child again and learn a new language. My expertise is useless there. Sweden is not interested in Iraq—what is Iraq to Sweden? But in the U.S. I would find a hundred organizations interested in hiring me. I have the numbers of nearly every member of the Iraqi government in my phone, I know them in person, they know me in person, I know their aides, I know how to get to them, and I believe this is something very valuable for the State Department. In America I would probably merge, some people would take me as a Cuban or as a Latino, not necessarily as a Middle Eastern. But in Sweden I would surely be taken as an outsider. We know each other a little now, Americans and Iraqis, even if it is a terrible situation. Sometimes we are talking, sometimes we are fighting, but at least this is a relationship. It is not something to throw away or burn. But America doesn't want me.

He looks at the interviewer as if he's just been asked one final question.

Betrayed? Not really. I have this nature—I don't expect a lot from people. I always assume the better but don't expect a lot. Not betrayed, no, not disappointed. I can never blame the Americans alone. It's the Iraqis who destroyed their country, with the help of the Americans, under the American eye. (*He is looking beyond the interviewer toward something in the distance.*) Until this moment I dream about America.

Fade to black.